CONTENTS

TRYING TRIATHLONS

For some racers, one sport just isn't enough. In that case, a triathlon is just the right race! Made up of three parts, most commonly swimming, biking, and running, triathlons come in many distances, or lengths. Brave people looking for an extra-long triathlon often pick an Ironman race.

RACE FOR YOUR LIFE!

IRONMAN TRIATHLON

BY KATE MIKOLEY

HOT TOPICS

Please visit our website, www.garethstevens.com. For a free color catalog of all our high-quality books, call toll free 1-800-542-2595 or fax 1-877-542-2596.

Cataloging-in-Publication Data

Names: Mikoley, Kate.
Title: Ironman triathlon / Kate Mikoley.
Description: New York : Gareth Stevens Publishing, 2021. | Series: Race for your life! | Includes glossary and index.
Identifiers: ISBN 9781538258989 (pbk.) | ISBN 9781538259009 (library bound) | ISBN 9781538258996 (6 pack)
Subjects: LCSH: Triathlon–History–Juvenile literature. | Triathlon–Training–Juvenile literature.
Classification: LCC GV1060.73 M57 2021 | DDC 796.42'57–dc23

First Edition

Published in 2021 by
Gareth Stevens Publishing
111 East 14th Street, Suite 349
New York, NY 10003

Designer: Laura Bowen
Editor: Kate Mikoley

Photo credits: Cover, pp. 1–32 (texture) Chatham172/Shutterstock.com; Cover, pp. 1 (triathlete) Mark Runnacles/Stringer/Getty Images Europe/Getty Images; p. 5 (runner) Mike Harrington/Stone/Getty Images Plus/Getty Images; p. 5 (biker) Tim Tadder/Corbis/Getty Images Plus/Getty Images; p. 5 (swimmer) AMR Image/E+/Getty Images; p. 7 FatCamera/E+/Getty Images; pp. 9, 27 picture alliance/Contributor/picture alliance/Getty Images; p. 11 Christian Petersen/Staff/Getty Images North America/Getty Images; p. 13 Donald Miralle/Contributor/Sports Illustrated/Getty Images; p. 15 MediaNews Group/Boulder Daily Camera via Getty Images/Contributor/MediaNews Group RM/Getty Images; pp. 17, 19 Tom Pennington/Staff/Getty Images North America/Getty Images; p. 21 NurPhoto/Contributor/NurPhoto/Getty Images; p. 23 Hugo Ortu±o Sußrez/Contributor/Moment Editorial/Getty Images; p. 25 Sean M. Haffey/Staff/Getty Images North America/Getty Images; p. 29 Kohjiro Kinno/Contributor/Sports Illustrated/Getty Images.

Printed in the United States of America

CPSIA compliance information: Batch #CS20GS: For further information contact Gareth Stevens, New York, New York at 1-800-542-2595.

FEARLESS FACTS

Ironman events are considered endurance races. Endurance means having the power to do something hard for a long time.

Triathlons start with swimming. Next is biking, and then running. An Olympic triathlon is a 0.9-mile (1.5 km) swim, a 24.9-mile (40 km) bike ride, and a 6.2-mile (10 km) run. That might seem like a long race, but an Ironman is longer!

FEARLESS FACTS

A person who takes part in sports or other activities having to do with exercise is called an athlete. A person who does triathlons is a triathlete.

BREAKING IT DOWN

Ironman triathlons are held all over the world, all year round. The races start with a 2.4-mile (3.9 km) swim. Next comes the 112-mile (180.2 km) bike ride. Lastly, athletes complete a 26.2-mile (42.2 km) run.

FEARLESS FACTS

A marathon is a 26.2-mile (42.2 km) running race. A lot of training goes into finishing a marathon. Ironman racers run a full marathon after already swimming and biking!

THE SWIM

The swimming section, or part, of an Ironman could be in an ocean, lake, bay, or other body of water. If a lot of people are racing, the water might get choppy. This can make it harder to swim fast.

FEARLESS FACTS

If the water is cold, racers may wear a piece of clothing called a wet suit during the swim. It's made of rubber and keeps their bodies warm.

THE BIKE RIDE

After the swim, racers leave the water and find their bike. Commonly, rows of bikes line an area called the **transition** area. Racers may quickly change and put on shoes before starting the biking part of the race.

FEARLESS FACTS

Ironman racers must wear helmets during the biking section of the race.

THE RUN

After a hard swim and bike ride, it's time for racers to run the marathon. Like the biking section, the run often takes place on **paved** roads. All Ironman courses, or paths, are a bit different, so runners may face hills or other **challenges**.

FEARLESS FACTS

When changing from the bike to running, some triathletes get pains in their legs called cramps. These happen when **muscles** tighten.

TRANSITION TIME

Racers don't want to waste any time between the different sections of the race. One thing that can make transitions quicker is a tri-suit. This is a special piece of clothing that can be worn for all three parts of the race.

FEARLESS FACTS

A tri-suit is made of a special **material** that dries quickly, so you won't stay too wet after the swim.

Even with a tri-suit, racers still must change some of their gear during transitions. Triathletes wear special shoes that clip onto their bike's **pedals** for the biking part of the race. Then, they have to be able to quickly change into their running shoes.

FEARLESS FACTS

Racers also use the transitions as a time to drink water. Lots of triathletes also drink sports drinks and eat special foods to keep their strength up.

IRONMAN HISTORY

The first **official** triathlon happened in California in 1974. One of the finishers was a U.S. Navy officer named John Collins. A few years later, Collins and his wife Judy wanted to hold their own triathlon in Hawaii, where they lived.

FEARLESS FACTS

The Collinses wanted a long race. The name came from when they were planning it. John told Judy, "Whoever finishes first, we'll call him the Iron Man."

On February 18, 1978, the Collinses held their event, the Hawaiian Iron Man Triathlon. This first event had 15 racers and was the same distance as today's Ironman races. In 1980, the race was shown on TV. Soon, more people wanted to do it!

FEARLESS FACTS

Today, there are Ironman events held on every **continent** except Antarctica. The Ironman World Championships are held in Hawaii.

TIME TO TRAIN

Unlike other kinds of races, training for a triathlon is like training for three different races. The training takes a lot of time and hard work. Some people spend a whole year working on their swimming, biking, and running skills.

FEARLESS FACTS

Someone might be a great swimmer in a pool, but open water is different. Athletes often train outdoors to practice swimming in cold water or with a current, or tide.

MANY MILES

Altogether, an Ironman triathlon is 140.6 miles (226.3 km). The fastest racers often finish in less than nine hours. Most people take closer to 12 or 13 hours. Today, there's also a shorter race, Ironman 70.3. It's half the distance of a regular Ironman.

FEARLESS FACTS

Some people want even longer triathlons. In 1998 there was a triathlon 20 times as long as an Ironman! The winner took more than 18 days to finish.

WOULD YOU TRY IT?

Would you race in an Ironman event? If you think it's something you want to do someday, you can start practicing now. Learn about bike safety and practice following the rules of the road. Find out if your school or community has swimming or running teams you can join.

FEARLESS FACTS

You might not be ready for an Ironman triathlon yet, but there are some shorter triathlons for kids. Ask an adult to help you find out if there's one near where you live.

GEAR CHECKLIST

TRI-SUIT

SWIMMING GOGGLES

BIKE HELMET

BIKE SHOES

RUNNING SHOES

WATER, SPORTS DRINKS, AND FOOD

SUNBLOCK

SUNGLASSES

FOR MORE INFORMATION

BOOKS

Poletti, Frances and Kristina Yee. *The Girl Who Ran: Bobbi Gibb, the First Woman to Run the Boston Marathon.* Seattle, WA: Compendium Inc., 2017.

Shea, Therese. *All About Bicycles*. New York, NY: Britannica Educational Publishing, 2017.

Vanden Branden, Claire. *Swimming.* Minneapolis, MN: Pop!, 2020.

WEBSITES

Ironman
www.ironman.com
Find out more about these cool races on the official Ironman website.

Swimming
www.dkfindout.com/us/sports/swimming/
Get more facts about swimming here.

What Is a Triathlon?
www.wonderopolis.org/wonder/what-is-a-triathlon
Head to this website to learn more about triathlons.

GLOSSARY

challenge: a test of abilities

continent: one of Earth's seven great landmasses

goggles: special glasses that guard the eyes

material: something used to make something, such as a fabric

muscle: one of the parts of the body that allow movement

official: having the support of a group

paved: covered with matter to form a hard, level surface like a road

pedal: a flat object attached to a bike that you push with your foot to make the bike move

transition: to change from one thing to another

INDEX